The Seasons

Edited by John N. Serio • Illustrated by Robert Crockett

STERLING CHILDREN'S BOOKS
New York

To my *four seasons: Faye, Alisa, Alexis, and Andrew;*
and to Sheila Barry, again –J.N.S.

To Victoria, William, and Lynn –R.C.

STERLING CHILDREN'S BOOKS
New York

An Imprint of Sterling Publishing
387 Park Avenue South
New York, NY 10016

This new edition published in 2014 by Sterling Publishing Co., Inc.
Originally published in 2005 by Sterling Publishing Co., Inc.

© 2005 by Magnolia Editions Limited
Introduction © 2005 by John N. Serio
Illustrations © 2005 by Robert Crockett

ISBN 978-1-4549-1347-4

Distributed in Canada by Sterling Publishing
c/o Canadian Manda Group, 165 Dufferin Street
Toronto, Ontario, Canada M6K 3H6

For information about custom editions, special sales, and premium and corporate purchases,
please contact Sterling Special Sales at 800-805-5489 or specialsales@sterlingpublishing.com

Manufactured in China
Lot #:
2 4 6 8 10 9 7 5 3 1
05/14

www.sterlingpublishing.com/kids

Contents

Introduction

Blue. Orange. White. Green.
Just the colors themselves suggest the four seasons. Summer is a time of endless blue skies and warmth, freedom and playfulness. Autumn offers a brilliant kaleidoscope of painted landscapes. Blanketed in a white layer of freshly fallen snow, cities and country fields alike take on a new charm in winter. In spring, lawns turn seemingly overnight from a dull brown to a vibrant green, and trees and flowers, surging with new life, explode into a rainbow of colors.

Poets have always turned to the seasons to celebrate their attractive features. For Nikki Giovanni, summer is the season when "you can eat fresh corn" and "go barefooted / and be warm." For the six-year-old Hilda Conkling, autumn is when she can become "queen of yellow leaves and brown" and build a magical "ring of leaves" to stay warm. William Shakespeare reminds us that when "icicles hang by the wall" and "Marian's nose looks red and raw," we can still find comfort in a cozy kitchen, where "roasted crabs [crab apples] hiss in the bowl." And e. e. cummings captures the sheer joy of spring when the world has become "mud-luscious" and "puddle-wonderful."

In a humorous vein, Robert Louis Stevenson offers a traditional complaint about summer: because the days are longer, children have to go to bed when there is still plenty of daylight. It's unfair! he cries. The "scarlet gown" of the fields in autumn inspires Emily Dickinson to put on a "trinket," a bit of her own jewelry. Walking in winter's snow, says Elinor Wylie, is like walking on "velvet shoes"—you can hear the silence. Walter de la Mare marvels at a mere snowflake: it is powerful enough to turn a forest into a blank wilderness, yet delicate enough, if you were just to breathe on it, to "vanish / Instantly!" With its long column of words, William Carlos Williams' "The Locust Tree in Flower" (p. 47) looks like a tree branch. The poem's stumbling language mimics nature's struggle to come back to life after winter's sleep. We are thrilled that the sweet blossoms of May return—"again."

There is even a form of poetry traditionally built around the seasons. It is called haiku and was developed by the Japanese hundreds of years ago. Only three lines in length, these short poems release a strong emotion, usually by an association with a seasonal image. Often the time of year is not even mentioned, but rather implied: "a croaking frog" suggests summer; "a crow on a branch" means autumn; "white" stands for winter; "cherry blossom" conveys spring. Like a landscape painting, each haiku captures an instant in time. Because they are so brief and suggestive, each haiku depends on the reader to complete it in his or her own imagination. Haiku are fun to write. An easy way to do it is to compose three lines—the first with five syllables, the next with seven, and the last with five syllables. Remember: limit yourself to what you can see, hear, smell, taste, or touch. Try it!

Poets can also show us two sides to a season. Thomas Hood's delightful poem about November emphasizes the season's discomfort and dreariness. Taking his cue from the word "November," he humorously titles the poem "No!" (p. 21): "No warmth, no cheerfulness, no healthful ease, / . . . No fruits, no flowers, no leaves, no birds, / November!" But John Keats presents an opposite view. In "To Autumn" (p. 22), Keats cherishes autumn as the "Season of mists and mellow fruitfulness"—the season of the harvest, when fruit, vegetables, and nuts swell with ripeness. Although one normally associates the music of birds with spring, Keats says that autumn, too, has its music: full-grown lambs cry, crickets sing, robins whistle, and "gathering swallows twitter in the skies."

Too often we take the seasons for granted, as if we are all too familiar with them. But A. E. Housman shocks us into awareness, as only poets can do, of how few of the seasons we actually experience in our lifetime. In "Loveliest of trees, the cherry now" (p. 44), the twenty-year-old speaker realizes that he has seen spring only twenty times. If he were to live till age seventy (an average lifespan), he would have only fifty more opportunities to experience spring. "And since to look at things in bloom / Fifty springs are little room," he decides to take the time to appreciate the loveliness of the cherry blossoms. The way in which the white blossoms resemble snow at the end of the poem emphasizes their short-lived nature. (How many times have you seen spring?)

Seasons also provide us with a means to give voice to our deepest feelings and thoughts. Robert Frost in "Tree at My Window" (not included here) notices that the tree outside his bedroom window blows and tosses in the wind, just as he turns and tosses in his troubled sleep:

> *That day she put our heads together,*
> *Fate had her imagination about her,*
> *Your head so much concerned with outer,*
> *Mine with inner, weather.*

By "inner weather" Frost means human feelings. Poets use the outer weather of nature, often depicted in a particular season, to communicate a human theme. Nikki Giovanni in "Knoxville, Tennessee" (p. 16) uses the comfort, freedom, and warmth of summertime to convey something much more meaningful: the sense of security and love she feels when surrounded by family and friends. Although he describes an old dog, James S. Tippett expresses the sense of laziness we all experience while waiting out the blazing heat of a summer's afternoon (p. 9). Langston Hughes selects the imagery of a barren winter landscape to emphasize the importance of holding fast to our dreams (p. 36). The magic of one word in Walt Whitman's "The First Dandelion" (p. 40) turns a description of a weed into something hopeful: the face of spring's first dandelion is "trustful."

Sometimes, as in Frost's "Dust of Snow" (p. 31), a reversal can take place and the outer weather can change our outlook. For an unknown reason, the speaker starts out the day feeling glum and unhappy. A funny occurrence—a lump of snow falling from a tree on him as he walks through the woods—completely alters his mood. This humorous incident—almost a deliberate action, by the way, on the part of a crow—shakes him out of his depression and saves the day.

Bliss Carman and William Wordsworth also focus on this aspect of how seasonal weather can affect our mood. The flaming colors of autumn in "A Vagabond Song"(p. 26) ignite Carman's spirit and he feels excitement in the air. For a reason he cannot explain—"There is something in the autumn that is native to my blood"—fall arouses the wanderlust in him, the motivation to travel and see more of the world. The flaming colors of the leaves become a drumbeat to his spirit.

In "I Wandered Lonely As a Cloud" (p. 46), Wordsworth begins his springtime trek through the hills feeling aimless and lonely. Suddenly he comes upon a field containing thousands of golden daffodils "Fluttering and dancing in the breeze," and he is made joyful by their company. But Wordsworth goes even further, for this moment in spring stays with him forever. Often, when just lying on his couch, perhaps in the middle of winter, the image of the scene flashes across his imagination, and his heart, once again, fills with pleasure as it "dances with the daffodils."

There is yet another value associated with seasons. They represent stages in human life. Just as the seasons come to us as a result of the earth's long journey around the sun, so too do they come to represent the different phases we pass through in our own journey through life.

Summer is the period of adulthood, the prime time of life, when we exhibit vigor, strength, health, and confidence. Autumn is a more somber stage, when we are settled in life and can take the time to reflect on the past and on the future. As nature withdraws into hibernation or death, winter presents us with an image of our own end or mortality, causing us to consider more deeply the meaning of family, friends, and work. Spring, with its resurgence of new life and energy, represents youth, vitality, and rebirth, and it inspires renewed energy, excitement, and anticipation.

William Butler Yeats uses this characteristic of the seasons to communicate a period in the speaker's life. The setting of "The Wild Swans at Coole" (p. 24; Coole is the name of a private country park in Ireland) is autumn. But the poem implies something greater: the "autumn" of the speaker's life. As Yeats describes the swans, they represent an ideal of eternal youth and perfection, something mortal humans cannot possess. Although many years have gone by since the speaker first counted them, the swans seem not to have changed: "Their hearts have not grown old." But the speaker has changed. This makes him reflect on his own end, but he does so in a surprisingly mystical manner. He relates the eternal quality of the swans to his own passing. After dying, he will "awake some day" to wonder at the beautiful mystery of life.

The four seasons—summer, autumn, winter, spring—are each dramatic in their own way. Poets value them not only for their natural splendor but also for the way they help express our deepest feelings, thoughts, and desires. The cycle of the seasons reveals the cycle of our lives.

Blue. Orange. White. Green.

Again.

Poems of
Summer

HAIKU

Daybreak in Summer

Ryota (1719–1787)

This lovely summer morn
Hushed is the voice of every man
In wonder at the dawn.

Clouds and Poppies

Kwanrai (1748–1817)

Below, the poppies red;
And driving o'er the summer sky
The white clouds overhead.

A Summer Landscape

Banko (before 1800; dates unknown)

How cool the cattle seem!
They love to swish their tails and stand
Knee-deep within the stream.

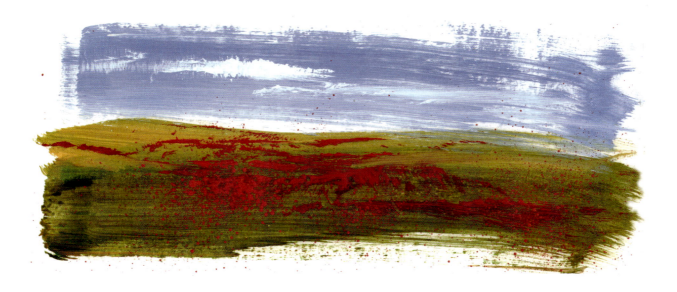

Sunning

James S. Tippett (1885–1958)

An author of children's poetry and short stories, Tippett also wrote books on education and environmental conservation. He was born in Missouri and lived most of his life in North Carolina, so he knew firsthand the effects of the summer heat. He uses an endearing old dog to show how lazy you can become when the heat of the sun saps your physical energies. Old Dog is content just to dream about being active in such heat. Even the lengths of the lines, when describing the dog's actions, are shorter to reflect his lack of energy.

Old Dog lay in the summer sun
Much too lazy to rise and run.
He flapped an ear
At a buzzing fly.
He winked a half opened
Sleepy eye.
He scratched himself
On an itching spot,
As he dozed on the porch
Where the sun was hot.
He whimpered a bit
From force of habit
While he lazily dreamed
Of chasing a rabbit.
But Old Dog happily lay in the sun
Much too lazy to rise and run.

Henry Wadsworth Longfellow (1807–1882)

*One of the most admired poets of the nineteenth century,
Longfellow popularized American legends in such poems
as "Paul Revere's Ride" and "The Song of Hiawatha." He
grew up in Portland, Maine, and taught modern languages
at Harvard. In 1854, he gave up his professorship to devote
himself exclusively to writing. Living in Boston, which can
be uncomfortably hot and humid in the summer, Longfellow
must have welcomed a refreshing downpour. Notice how in
this poem he communicates the beauty of the rain, not by its
cooling effect, but by its sound.*

How beautiful is the rain!
After the dust and heat,
In the broad and fiery street,
In the narrow lane,
How beautiful is the rain!

How it clatters along the roofs,
Like the tramp of hoofs!
How it gushes and struggles out
From the throat of the overflowing spout!

Across the window-pane
It pours and pours;
And swift and wide,
With a muddy tide,
Like a river down the gutter roars
The rain, the welcome rain!

Bed in Summer

Robert Louis Stevenson (1850–1894)

Most adults know the works of Stevenson, who was born in Edinburgh, Scotland, through his tales of adventure, such as Treasure Island *and* Kidnapped, *or his horror story,* The Strange Case of Dr. Jekyll and Mr. Hyde. *But for over 100 years, children have known Stevenson as the author of* A Child's Garden of Verses, *from which the following poem is taken. As a child, Stevenson was sickly, and he often amused himself writing poems and stories. As an adult, he struggled with tuberculosis. Needing a better climate for his health, he moved in 1889 to Samoa, an island in the South Seas. He quickly gained the affection of the natives, who called him Tusitala, "teller of tales," and at his request, when he died he was buried there.*

In winter I get up at night
And dress by yellow candle-light.
In summer, quite the other way,
I have to go to bed by day.

I have to go to bed and see
The birds still hopping on the tree,
Or hear the grown-up people's feet
Still going past me in the street.

And does it not seem hard to you,
When all the sky is clear and blue,
And I should like so much to play,
To have to go to bed by day?

Sumer is icumen in

Anonymous (thirteenth-century song)

*Over the centuries, the English language has undergone
dramatic changes. This poem is written in Middle English
(1100–1450), and it is one of the earliest recorded songs in
our language. It is in the form of a round such as "Row, Row,
Row Your Boat." The song of the cuckoo traditionally marked
the end of winter and the beginning of spring. Try reading
the poem aloud in the original and you will be speaking the
way people did nearly 1,000 years ago!*

Sumer is icumen in,
    Lhude sing, cuccu!
Groweth sed and bloweth med
    And springeth the wude nu.
      Sing, cuccu!

Awe bleteth after lomb,
    Lhouth after calve cu,
Bulluc sterteth, bucke verteth—
    Murie sing, cuccu!
      Cuccu, cuccu.
    Wel singes thu, cuccu.
    Ne swik thu never nu!

Sing cuccu nu! Sing cuccu!
Sing cuccu! Sing cuccu nu!

Summer is Coming

Summer is coming in,
 Loud sing, cuckoo!
Groweth seed and bloweth meadow
 And springeth the wood new.
  Sing, cuckoo!

Ewe bleateth after lamb,
 Loweth after calf cow,
Bullock starteth, buck farteth—
 Merrily sing, cuckoo!
  Cuckoo, cuckoo.
 Well singest thou, cuckoo.
 Now stop thou never no!

Sing, cuckoo now! Sing, cuckoo!
Sing, cuckoo! Sing, cuckoo, now!

maggie and milly and molly and may

e. e. cummings (1894–1962)

*edward estlin cummings had great fun with the English language, as we
can see even in the way he spelled his name, using only lowercase letters.
He was born in Cambridge, Massachusetts, and graduated from Harvard.
A new invention, the typewriter, influenced the visual arrangement of
his poems. He designed his poems on the page the way he wanted them to
look in print. His original style gave new life to words and allowed him to
create unusual effects such as the tender feelings evoked in this charming
poem of discovery about a day at the beach.*

maggie and milly and molly and may
went down to the beach (to play one day)

and maggie discovered a shell that sang
so sweetly she couldn't remember her troubles, and

milly befriended a stranded star
whose rays five languid fingers were;

and molly was chased by a horrible thing
which raced sideways while blowing bubbles: and

may came home with a smooth round stone
as small as a world and as large as alone.

For whatever we lose(like a you or a me)
it's always ourselves we find in the sea

Knoxville, Tennessee

Nikki Giovanni (1943–)

An African American poet who has used her writing to promote civil rights and equality, Giovanni was born in Knoxville, Tennessee. Although her poetry is often about the experience of being a black American, her emphasis is on the individual, whose potential can create changes in oneself and thus in others. With its use of traditional food and localized setting, this poem speaks of the love and warmth we all feel when surrounded by family and friends.

I always like summer
best
you can eat fresh corn
from daddy's garden
and okra
and greens
and cabbage
and lots of
barbecue
and buttermilk
and homemade ice-cream
at the church picnic
and listen to
gospel music
outside
at the church
homecoming
and go to the mountains with
your grandmother
and go barefooted
and be warm
all the time
not only when you go to bed
and sleep

Summer Song

John Ciardi (1916–1986)

Ciardi had many talents. He was well known as a translator, literary critic, editor, and teacher, but he was also a poet, composing over four dozen books of poetry. With such titles as Blabberhead, Bobble-Bud & Spade, *and* The Man Who Sang the Sillies, *from which "Summer Song" is taken, Ciardi often wrote humorous verse to encourage a love of poetry in children. He was born in Boston and taught for many years at Rutgers University.*

By the sand between my toes,
By the waves behind my ears,
By the sunburn on my nose,
By the little salty tears
That make rainbows in the sun
When I squeeze my eyes and run,
By the way the seagulls screech,
Guess where I am? *At the . . . . . !*
By the way the children shout
Guess what happened? *School is . . . . . !*
By the way I sing this song
Guess if summer lasts too long:
You must answer Right or . . . . . !

Poems of
Autumn

HAIKU

Sweeping Up Fallen Maple Leaves

Ryota (1719–1787)

’Tis evening calm and clear,
The rustling of the maple leaves
Is all the sound I hear.

An Autumn Evening

Kikaku (1661–1707)

The autumn day is done,
A single solitary owl
Smiles at the setting sun.

A Glimpse of Sun

Shôsan (1718–1801)

Like autumn leaves, the sky
Still scatters sunshine here and there,
Though storm clouds gather nigh.

Autumn Song

Hilda Conkling (1910–1986)

Conkling was a child wonder when she started composing poetry at age four and published her first book, Poems by a Little Girl, *at age twelve. Before she could write, she would tell her poems to her mother, who would write them down, so it is no surprise that she dedicated her first book to her mother:*

> *I have a dream for you, Mother,*
> *Like a soft thick fringe to hide your eyes.*
> *I have a surprise for you, Mother,*
> *Shaped like a strange butterfly.*
> *I have found a way of thinking*
> *To make you happy;*
> *I have made a song and a poem*
> *All twisted into one.*
> *If I sing, you listen;*
> *If I think, you know. . . .*

Born in Northampton, Massachusetts, Conkling uses her natural surroundings in a highly imaginative way, creating a poetic magic, as in this poem, composed at age six.

I made a ring of leaves
On the autumn grass:
I was a fairy queen all day.
Inside the ring, the wind wore sandals
Not to make a noise of going.
The caterpillars, like little snow men,
Had wound themselves in their winter coats.
The hands of the trees were bare
And their fingers fluttered.
I was a queen of yellow leaves and brown,
And the redness of my fairy ring
Kept me warm.

For the wind blew near,
Though he made no noise of going,
And I hadn't a close-made wrap
Like the caterpillars.
Even a queen of fairies can be cold
When summer is forgotten and gone!
Keep me warm, red leaves;
Don't let the frost tiptoe into my ring
On the magic grass!

No!

Thomas Hood (1799–1845)

Born in London, England, Hood is best remembered for his poems of humor and social concern. One of his most popular poems is "The Song of the Shirt," which is about the terrible working conditions of women who must "Stitch! stitch! stitch!" all day in a shirt factory. Like other nineteenth-century authors, Hood usually writes in a conventional style, using a clear pattern of rhythm and rhyme, but "No!" has a remarkably modern sound to it. It cannot hide Hood's love of the comic.

No sun—no moon!
No morn—no noon—
No dawn—no dusk—no proper time of day—
  No sky—no earthly view—
  No distance looking blue—
No road—no street—no "t'other side the way"—
  No end to any Row—
  No indications where the Crescents go—
  No top to any steeple—
No recognitions of familiar people—
  No courtesies for showing 'em—
  No knowing 'em!—
No travelling at all—no locomotion,
No inkling of the way—no notion—
  "No go"—by land or ocean—
  No mail—no post—
  No news from any foreign coast—
No Park—no Ring—no afternoon gentility—
  No company—no nobility—
No warmth, no cheerfulness, no healthful ease,
  No comfortable feel in any member—
No shade, no shine, no butterflies, no bees,
  No fruits, no flowers, no leaves, no birds,
    November!

Row . . . Crescents—*a row of houses built in the inner form of the crescent moon.*

No Park—no Ring—*The Ring in Hyde Park in London was a fashionable place for horseback riding.*

To Autumn

John Keats (1795–1821)

Although Keats, who was born in London, England, lived only a short time, he became one of the greatest poets of the English language. His poems are deeply felt expressions of the beauty, joy, and sometimes the heartache of life. His naturally flowing verse is musical and dignified. It contains rich and vivid description that stimulates all our senses, so that we share the experience of the poem. Unfortunately, he lived a tragically brief life. His father was killed in a horse accident when Keats was eight and his mother died of tuberculosis when he was fourteen. Although Keats studied medicine, he gave it up to devote himself to poetry. While caring for his brother Tom, who died in 1818 of tuberculosis, Keats contracted the disease. During the next year, he composed his greatest poetry, but his poor health took its toll. In search of a better climate, he traveled to Italy, where he died at age twenty-five. He was buried in Rome.

"To Autumn" celebrates the often-unnoticed beauty of fall. In the first stanza, Keats sees autumn as a friend helping nature's fruits ripen and late flowers bloom; in the second, he imagines the season as a woman, leisurely resting from the work of harvesting; and in the third stanza, he evokes, not the traditional sights of autumn, but its sounds.

1

Season of mists and mellow fruitfulness,
  Close bosom-friend of the maturing sun;
Conspiring with him how to load and bless
  With fruit the vines that round the thatch-eaves run;
To bend with apples the mossed cottage-trees,
  And fill all fruit with ripeness to the core;
    To swell the gourd, and plump the hazel shells
With a sweet kernel; to set budding more,
  And still more, later flowers for the bees,
  Until they think warm days will never cease,
    For Summer has o'er-brimmed their clammy cells.

conspiring—*to be in harmony*

thatch-eaves—*the part of a straw roof that hangs over the edge*

gourd—*plant that has a hard outer covering such as a squash or pumpkin*

hazel—*nuts*

o'er-brimmed—*overflowing*

2

Who hath not seen thee oft amid thy store?
    Sometimes whoever seeks abroad may find
Thee sitting careless on a granary floor,
    Thy hair soft-lifted by the winnowing wind;
Or on a half-reaped furrow sound asleep,
    Drowsed with the fume of poppies, while thy hook
      Spares the next swath and all its twinèd flowers:
And sometimes like a gleaner thou dost keep
    Steady thy laden head across a brook;
    Or by a cider-press, with patient look,
      Thou watchest the last oozings hours by hours.

3

Where are the songs of Spring? Aye, where are they?
    Think not of them, thou hast thy music too—
While barrèd clouds bloom the soft-dying day,
    And touch the stubble-plains with rosy hue;
Then in a wailful choir the small gnats mourn
    Among the river sallows, borne aloft
      Or sinking as the light wind lives or dies;
And full-grown lambs loud bleat from hilly bourn;
    Hedge crickets sing; and now with treble soft
    The redbreast whistles from a garden-croft;
      And gathering swallows twitter in the skies.

store—*a large quantity, abundance*

granary—*storehouse for grain*

winnowing—*technique to separate grain from its covering*

hook—*scythe or cutting tool*

twinèd—*twisted together*

gleaner— *one who gathers grain or other produce left by reapers*

laden—*heavy*

sallows—*low-lying willows*

bourn—*usually stream; here region*

croft—*an enclosed plot of farmland*

The Wild Swans at Coole

W. B. Yeats (1865–1939)

Considered Ireland's best poet, Yeats was born in Dublin. At first he wanted to be a painter, like his father, but then decided to be a poet. His early poems sounded old-fashioned—dreamy tales of Irish folklore and legends. But then his style changed to become more direct, specific, and realistic, as in this poem about fifty-nine swans. Yeats worked hard to support Irish nationalism and Irish culture, and even served as a Senator of the Irish Free State. In 1923, he won the Nobel Prize in Literature, the most notable of all awards.

The trees are in their autumn beauty,
The woodland paths are dry,
Under the October twilight the water
Mirrors a still sky;
Upon the brimming water among the stones
Are nine-and-fifty swans.

The nineteenth autumn has come upon me
Since I first made my count;
I saw, before I had well finished,
All suddenly mount
And scatter wheeling in great broken rings
Upon their clamorous wings.

I have looked upon those brilliant creatures,
And now my heart is sore.
All's changed since I, hearing at twilight,
The first time on this shore,
The bell-beat of their wings above my head,
Trod with a lighter tread.

Unwearied still, lover by lover,
They paddle in the cold
Companionable streams or climb the air;
Their hearts have not grown old;
Passion or conquest, wander where they will,
Attend upon them still.

But now they drift on the still water,
Mysterious, beautiful;
Among what rushes will they build,
By what lake's edge or pool
Delight men's eyes when I awake some day
To find they have flown away?

Coole—*Coole Park, the country estate of Yeats' friend Lady Gregory in Galway, Ireland*

rushes—*reedy, wetland plants; cattails*

The morns are meeker than they were

Emily Dickinson (1830–1886)

With her unconventional style, Dickinson was fifty years ahead of her time. Only seven of her poems appeared in print during her lifetime. After her death, her sister discovered nearly 2,000 of them! Over 900 were neatly bound into sixty hand-sewn booklets, while others, written on scraps of paper, were stuffed into her bedroom dresser. Born in Amherst, Massachusetts, Dickinson attended local schools and had a normal social life, but as time went on she withdrew from society and dressed only in white. Her world became her house, family, and garden, but her thoughts were as large as the universe. She was a poetic genius.

The morns are meeker than they were,
The nuts are getting brown;
The berry's cheek is plumper,
The rose is out of town.

The maple wears a gayer scarf,
The field a scarlet gown.
Lest I should be old-fashioned,
I'll put a trinket on.

A Vagabond Song

Bliss Carman (1861–1929)

Carman is a Canadian poet, born in Fredericton, New Brunswick. He published over fifty volumes of poetry and became Canada's best-known poet. After getting degrees from New Brunswick, Edinburgh (Scotland), and Harvard, he worked for many years in the United States as an editor for literary magazines. Carman's poems are filled with vivid images, emotion, and delicate musical phrasing, as in this uplifting song about autumn.

There is something in the autumn that is native to my blood—
Touch of manner, hint of mood;
And my heart is like a rhyme,
With the yellow and the purple and the crimson keeping time.

The scarlet of the maples can shake me like a cry
Of bugles going by.
And my lonely spirit thrills
To see the frosty asters like a smoke upon the hills.

There is something in October sets the gypsy blood astir;
We must rise and follow her,
When from every hill of flame
She calls and calls each vagabond by name.

vagabond, gypsy—*a person who moves from place to place, a wanderer*

asters—*star-shaped wildflowers that bloom in fall*

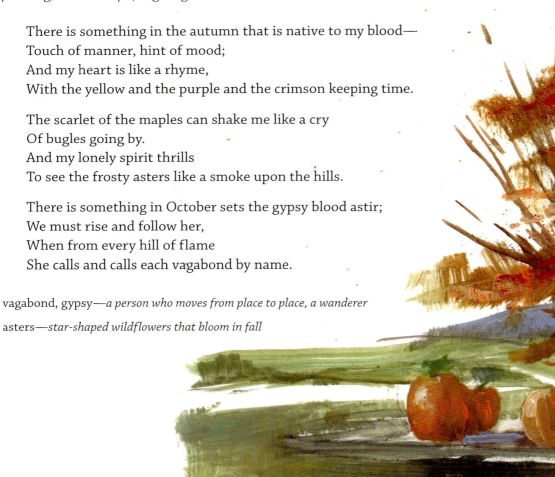

26

Poems of
Winter

HAIKU

Snow upon the Crows' Nests

Rimei (before 1800; dates unknown)

The heavy winter snows
Have capped with white the pine-tree tops,
Where sleep the big black crows.

A Heavy Snowfall

Riu (1662–1705)

Now all the world is white,
But where is one to find a spot
To view the lovely sight?

A Wintry Landscape

Issa (1763–1827)

The trees are frozen deep
In snowy garb, and now and then
A bird chirps in its sleep.

Velvet Shoes

Elinor Wylie (1885–1928)

Wylie was born in Somerville, New Jersey, and was both a poet and novelist. She was as well known for her beauty and daring personality as she was for her writing. Her verse, written in a traditional form, is limited in subject, but delicate and beautiful, as in this poem about the utter silence of walking in the snow.

Let us walk in the white snow
    In a soundless space;
With footsteps quiet and slow,
    At a tranquil pace,
    Under veils of white lace.

I shall go shod in silk,
    And you in wool,
White as a white cow's milk,
    More beautiful
    Than the breast of a gull.

We shall walk through the still town
    In a windless peace;
We shall step upon white down,
    Upon silver fleece,
    Upon softer than these.

We shall walk in velvet shoes:
    Wherever we go
Silence will fall like dews
    On white silence below.
    We shall walk in the snow.

shod—*usually, wearing shoes; here, any type of outer
   protection or covering*

down—*soft, fluffy feathers*

Dust of Snow

Robert Frost (1874–1963)

Perhaps because his poetry speaks so clearly to everyone, Frost is among America's most beloved poets. Although his poems are usually set in New England, he was born in San Francisco and did not move east until age eleven. After marrying his high-school sweetheart, he supported his family by farming and teaching, but he was a poet at heart. Like many struggling artists, he was not accepted at first. He wrote poems for nearly twenty years before he found a publisher, and he had to travel to England for that. But after his first two books appeared, he was celebrated as a major poet and he quickly returned to America. Frost is remarkable in the way he captures the spoken voice. His verse is simple and straightforward, yet deeply meaningful. He once said poetry "makes you remember what you didn't know you knew."

The way a crow
Shook down on me
The dust of snow
From a hemlock tree

Has given my heart
A change of mood
And saved some part
Of a day I had rued.

rued—*regretted*

When icicles hang by the wall

William Shakespeare (1564–1616)

Not much is known about Shakespeare's early life in Stratford, England, where he was born, but after he moved to London, he became the greatest playwright who ever lived. He wrote over thirty plays, including Romeo and Juliet, Macbeth, *and* Hamlet, *and even though 400 years have passed, they are still regularly performed all over the world. One of the elements that make his plays so exceptional is his use of language. Characters speak lines that express their deepest natures, but do so with pure poetry. Shakespeare also composed songs in his plays, such as this one about winter from* Love's Labor's Lost. *The vivid details capture not only the harsh coldness outside but also the cozy warmth inside.*

When icicles hang by the wall,
   And Dick the shepherd blows his nail,
And Tom bears logs into the hall,
   And milk comes frozen home in pail,
When blood is nipped and ways be foul,
Then nightly sings the staring owl—
        Tu-whit,
Tu-who, a merry note,
While greasy Joan doth keel the pot.

When all aloud the wind doth blow,
   And coughing drowns the parson's saw,
And birds sit brooding in the snow,
   And Marian's nose looks red and raw,
When roasted crabs hiss in the bowl,
Then nightly sings the staring owl—
        Tu-whit,
Tu-who, a merry note,
While greasy Joan doth keel the pot.

nail—*fingernails; here warming his hands*

keel—*cool by stirring*

saw—*moral statement or proverb*

crabs—*crab apples*

The winter evening settles down

T. S. Eliot (1888–1965)

A Nobel Prize winner, Thomas Stearns Eliot was the most famous poet of the first half of the twentieth century. Although his ancestors were originally from Massachusetts, he was born and raised in St. Louis. He attended Harvard and then studied abroad in France, Germany, and England, eventually becoming a British citizen in 1927. Much of his poetry is difficult and expresses his personal disappointment in a failed marriage and the anxiety of a generation that experienced, for the first time in history, a world at war (World War I). But many of Eliot's poems are quite positive and uplifting, as is this prelude, a term for a musical composition. The unexpected change in rhythm in the last line transforms an otherwise dull and common scene into something quite beautiful.

The winter evening settles down
With smell of steaks in passageways.
Six o'clock.
The burnt-out ends of smoky days.
And now a gusty shower wraps
The grimy scraps
Of withered leaves about your feet

And newspapers from vacant lots;
The showers beat
On broken blinds and chimney-pots,
And at the corner of the street
A lonely cab-horse steams and stamps.

And then the lighting of the lamps.

Winter Trees

William Carlos Williams (1883–1963)

Although a medical doctor all his life, specializing in pediatrics (babies), Williams is best known as a poet. He was born in Rutherford, New Jersey, and after his education, he returned to his hometown where he practiced medicine for forty years. Between appointments with patients, he would often jot down a poem on a prescription pad. Williams did not want poetry to sound flowery and artificial, so he wrote in the way people actually spoke. He believed ordinary objects, when seen rightly, have their own special quality. In this poem he reveals the dignity of trees in winter, for they have gained, lost, and now must patiently wait (again) for new leaves in the spring.

All the complicated details
of the attiring and
the disattiring are completed!
A liquid moon
moves gently among
the long branches.
Thus having prepared their buds
against a sure winter
the wise trees
stand sleeping in the cold.

attiring ... disattiring—*dressing ... undressing*

Dreams

Langston Hughes (1902–1967)

Hughes was born in Joplin, Missouri, and graduated from Lincoln University in Pennsylvania. He lived in several countries before settling in New York City, where he was instrumental in inspiring a black literary movement known as the Harlem Renaissance. His poems, usually set in the city, give voice to the despair, hope, and pride of being African American. By using the rhythms of the blues and jazz as well as the language of everyday black speech, Hughes pays tribute to his cultural heritage. This poem draws upon an image of winter to stress the importance of never giving up hope.

Hold fast to dreams　　　　Hold fast to dreams
For if dreams die　　　　　For when dreams go
Life is a broken-winged bird　Life is a barren field
That cannot fly.　　　　　Frozen with snow.

The Snowflake

Walter de la Mare (1873–1956)

Born in Kent, England, de la Mare began writing poetry in high school, where he founded a school paper. While continuing to write poetry, he worked in an office for an oil company until age thirty-five. Thereafter, with the help of his retirement income, he was able to devote the rest of his life to writing. De la Mare's poems are often marked by a delicate, fanciful, and dreamy atmosphere that brings to life the shadowy world between the real and unreal. Their musical rhythms and liquid phrasing create a soothing and mysterious effect, as in this poem about the fragile beauty of a snowflake.

Before I melt,
Come, look at me!
This lovely icy filigree!
Of a great forest
In one night
I make a wilderness
Of white:
By skyey cold
Of crystals made,
All softly, on
Your finger laid,
I pause, that you
My beauty see:
Breathe, and I vanish
Instantly!

Poems of
Spring

HAIKU

. . . .

A Cold Spring

Banrai (before 1800; dates unknown)

So chilly is the spring,
My little tea plants quite forget
They should be blossoming!

The Perfume of the Plums

Shôha (died in 1600)

So sweet the plum-trees smell;
Would that the brush that paints the flower
Could paint the scent as well!

Daffodils

Kikuriô (before 1800; dates unknown)

In spite of cold and chills
That usher in the early spring
We have the daffodils.

The First Dandelion

....

Walt Whitman (1819–1892)

No poet has had a greater impact on how poetry is written today than Whitman. When the first edition of Leaves of Grass *appeared in 1855, readers did not recognize it as poetry. His poems lacked traditional stanzas, rhyme, and meter. Today, we call that style free verse, and it is the form most used by poets now. Whitman liberated poetry in shape and content: he showed poets how to write in a style appropriate to the expression of the poem and to include all subject matter as equally important, such as the proud beauty of a dandelion. Whitman was born in rural Huntington, Long Island, and then moved as a child to Brooklyn, New York. Although he attended school for only five years, he read widely and earned his living as a printer, editor, and journalist. He expanded* Leaves of Grass *in eight editions, until it grew from a slim volume of twelve poems into a monumental book containing nearly 400.*

Simple and fresh and fair from winter's close emerging,
As if no artifice of fashion, business, politics, had ever been,
Forth from its sunny nook of shelter'd grass—innocent, golden, calm as the dawn,
The spring's first dandelion shows its trustful face.

Dear March, come in!

Emily Dickinson (1830–1886)

Dickinson thought metaphorically, that is, in language beyond the literal meaning. In this poem, the month of March becomes a long-awaited friend. Even in describing herself in a letter, Dickinson turned to vivid comparisons: "I . . . am small, like the wren; and my hair is bold, like the chestnut burr; and my eyes, like the sherry in the glass that the guest leaves."

Dear March, come in!
How glad I am!
I looked for you before.
Put down your hat—
You must have walked—
How out of breath you are!
Dear March, how are you?
And the rest?
Did you leave Nature well?
Oh, March, come right upstairs with me,
I have so much to tell!

in Just-

e. e. cummings (1894–1962)

In this poem, we can see more of cummings' wordplay, where made-up words such as "mud-luscious" and ungrammatical expressions such as "eddieandbill" express perfectly the joy and companionship children experience in spring. The unusual arrangement, with combined words, spaces between words, and single words as whole lines, teaches us to read the poem at a varying tempo, as if it were a musical score.

in Just-
spring   when the world is mud-
luscious the little
lame balloonman

whistles   far   and wee

and eddieandbill come
running from marbles and
piracies and it's
spring

when the world is puddle-wonderful

the queer
old balloonman whistles
far   and   wee
and bettyandisbel come dancing

from hop-scotch and jump-rope and

it's
spring
and
    the

                goat-footed

balloonMan   whistles
far
and
wee

goat-footed / balloonman—*the description recalls Pan, the god of shepherds and flocks in Greek mythology who was half man and half goat and who played the Pan-pipe, a flute-like instrument made of reeds.*

Loveliest of trees, the cherry now

A. E. Housman (1859–1936)

A professor of Latin at several universities in England, where he was born, Alfred Edward Housman was not only a classical scholar but also a poet. Although he published only two slim volumes, his poems are remarkable for their compactness and directness. His themes, as in this poem, are usually about the beauty of the English countryside and the brevity of life. Using a traditional style, his short poems are rich in suggestive power, as in the way the preciousness of life is conveyed by springtime blossoms that in their whiteness resemble snow.

Loveliest of trees, the cherry now
Is hung with bloom along the bough,
And stands about the woodland ride
Wearing white for Eastertide.

Now, of my threescore years and ten,
Twenty will not come again,
And take from seventy springs a score,
It only leaves me fifty more.

And since to look at things in bloom
Fifty springs are little room,
About the woodlands I will go
To see the cherry hung with snow.

threescore years and ten—*a "score" is 20 years; thus, 70 years, an average lifespan*

Depression before Spring

Wallace Stevens (1879–1955)

A successful businessman, Stevens is one of the most prominent poets of the twentieth century. He was born in Reading, Pennsylvania, and was educated at Harvard. He worked as a lawyer for the Hartford Accident and Indemnity Company in Hartford, Connecticut, and eventually became a vice president. He never retired, but all along composed some of the most beautiful and engaging poems in our language. Stevens often writes about the process of poetry, as in this poem, which humorously complains about the lack of poetic inspiration, symbolized by the absent song of the dove, as the rooster announces the dawn of a new season.

The cock crows
But no queen rises.

The hair of my blonde
Is dazzling,
As the spittle of cows
Threading the wind.

Ho! Ho!

But ki-ki-ri-ki
Brings no rou-cou,
No rou-cou-cou.

But no queen comes
In slipper green.

cock—*rooster*

spittle—*spit*

ki-ki-ri-ki—*the sound of a rooster welcoming the dawn of a new day*

rou-cou-cou—*the song of a mourning dove*

I Wandered Lonely As a Cloud

William Wordsworth (1770–1850)

Simply by believing that poetry should be written in the language spoken by ordinary people, Wordsworth started a poetic revolution. He inspired a new movement called Romanticism, which celebrates nature, the value of each individual, and the role of the imagination in life. Wordsworth grew up near England's beautiful Lake District, and the beauty of his surroundings stimulated him to write poems. This poem matches perfectly his definition of poetry as "the spontaneous overflow of powerful feelings . . . recollected in tranquillity."

I wandered lonely as a cloud
That floats on high o'er vales and hills,
When all at once I saw a crowd,
A host, of golden daffodils;
Beside the lake, beneath the trees,
Fluttering and dancing in the breeze.

Continuous as the stars that shine
And twinkle on the milky way,
They stretched in never-ending line
Along the margin of a bay:
Ten thousand saw I at a glance,
Tossing their heads in sprightly dance.

The waves beside them danced; but they
Outdid the sparkling waves in glee;
A poet could not but be gay,
In such a jocund company;
I gazed—and gazed—but little thought
What wealth the show to me had brought:

For oft, when on my couch I lie
In vacant or in pensive mood,
They flash upon that inward eye
Which is the bliss of solitude;
And then my heart with pleasure fills,
And dances with the daffodils.

vales—*valleys*

sprightly—*lively*

pensive—*thoughtful*

inward eye—*the imagination*

The Locust Tree in Flower

William Carlos Williams (1883–1963)

When Williams first published this poem, it was twice as long. This second version prunes the poem down to its essentials. Its sparse structure, with just one word to a line and gaps in grammar, mirrors both the look of the tree's branch and the difficult but beautiful process of rebirth. After a long, hard winter plants revive and come to new life, blossoming each spring once again.

Among
of
green

stiff
old
bright

broken
branch
come

white
sweet
May

again

Index